Galaxy Unveiled

Exploring the Wonders of the Solar System

Dharmendra Mishra

 Year of Publication: 2024 Publisher: DM Publication Author: Dharmendra Mishra

Introduction

Have you ever looked up at the night sky and wondered about the twinkling stars? Do you know what our Earth revolves around? Let's embark on an exciting journey through the solar system together. We will learn about the Sun, planets, moons, and much more. Do you know which is the biggest planet? Or which is the smallest? You will find answers to all these questions in this book.

You will learn how important the Sun is to us. You will also learn about the appearance of other planets and what they are like. So let's start our journey!

Table of Content

Milky Way

"Our solar system is a part of a larger cosmic structure called the Milky Way."

The term 'Milky Way' is used because when we look up at the night sky, we can see a faint, milky band of light. This band is composed of countless stars that are part of our galaxy. In ancient times, people thought this band resembled a river of milk, and hence, it was named the Milky Way."

Solar System

The Sun and Its Planetary Family Imagine we're in a very large city, and in the center, there's a huge fire burning. This fire is our "Sun". Around this fire, many small spheres are revolving, just like children revolve around their mother. These spheres are the planets of our solar system.
Our Sun is the center of our solar system, and eight planets revolve around it."

Planets of Our Solar System

- **Mercury**
- **Venus**
- **Earth**
- **Mars**
- **Jupiter**
- **Saturn**
- **Uranus**
- **Neptune**

The Sun's gravitational pull keeps these planets in their orbits. Earth, being the third planet from the Sun, is considered the most suitable for life.

interesting fact: Jupiter's gravity is so powerful that it pulls in small asteroids and comets, protecting Earth from them.

The Earth and Its Shape

The Earth is commonly perceived as a perfect sphere, however, in reality, it's not entirely round. It can be more accurately described as an oblate spheroid. This means that the Earth bulges slightly at the equator and is flattened at the poles. This shape is a result of the Earth's rotation on its axis. This rotation generates a centripetal force, causing matter at the equator to be pulled outwards.

Why is the Earth Round?

Gravity: The Earth's gravitational force pulls all matter towards its center. This is the primary reason why the Earth takes on a spherical shape. Rotation: The Earth rotates on its axis, causing the matter at the equator to be pulled outwards and the matter at the poles to be pulled inwards.

Why is the Earth's Shape Important?

- Day and Night: The Earth's rotation is the reason for day and night.
- Seasons: The Earth's tilt and its revolution around the Sun cause the seasons to change.

Formation of Oceans: The Earth's gravitational force causes the water in the oceans to collect on the Earth's surface.

Interesting Facts About Earth

- Age of the Earth: Scientists believe that the Earth is approximately 4.5 billion years old. Earth's Layers: The Earth is composed of three main layers: the crust, the mantle, and the core. Earth's Magnetic Field: The Earth has a magnetic field that protects us from harmful radiation from the Sun.
- Earth's Only Natural Satellite: The Moon is Earth's only natural satellite.

Moon

The Moon and Its Mysteries The Moon is the closest celestial body to us, being the Earth's natural satellite. Despite having no atmosphere or water, the Moon is of great significance to us. It is pulled by Earth's gravity, which is why the Moon always faces the Earth.

Interesting Facts About Moon

Interesting Fact: On the Moon, there are two sunrises and two sunsets every day, as the Moon's motion is due to its revolution around the Earth. Interesting Fact: The first human landing on the Moon is known as the "Apollo 11" mission. Neil Armstrong and Buzz Aldrin set foot on the Moon in 1969.

Mars

Signs of Life Mars is also called the "Red Planet" because its surface appears red due to the presence of oxide (rust). Scientists believe that there was once water on this planet, and perhaps even life. Various missions sent to Mars have revealed that the planet has a very thin atmosphere and very little water. Interesting fact: Mars has two small moons - Phobos and Deimos, which are very small and irregularly shaped.

Jupiter

Jupiter is the largest planet in the solar system. It is made of gas and has 79 known moons. Jupiter has a very large ring, called the "Galilean Ring". This planet has a very famous storm, called the "Great Red Spot", which has been raging for hundreds of years. Interesting fact: Jupiter's gravity is so strong that it attracts small comets and meteors, thereby protecting the Earth from their collisions.

Saturn

The Planet of Rings

Saturn is famous for its magnificent rings. These rings are composed of ice and rock. Saturn is the second largest planet in the solar system and has a total of 82 known moons. Saturn is so large that approximately 760 Earths could fit inside it. Interesting Fact: Saturn's atmosphere is very cold and the wind speeds here can reach up to 1800 kilometers per hour.

Mercury

The closest planet to the Sun, Mercury is super hot! It's also the smallest planet in our solar system.

Venus

Venus is often called Earth's twin because they are similar in size. But Venus is much hotter than Earth, and it spins in the opposite direction!

Uranus

Uranus is a very cold planet that spins on its side. It has 27 moons.

Neptune

The farthest planet from the Sun, Neptune is another ice giant. It's very windy on Neptune!

Fun Facts

Asteroids: Asteroids are large rocks that orbit the Sun, mostly between Mars and Jupiter.

Comets: Comets are like dirty snowballs that orbit the Sun. They can have long tails of gas and dust.

Why do all planets revolve around the Sun?

The Sun is very large and heavy, so it has a very strong pulling force, called gravity. This gravity pulls all the planets towards it and that's why they keep revolving around the Sun. Why is every planet different? Every planet is made up of different things and is at a different temperature. That's why every planet has its own color, size, and weather. Interesting fact: Venus has the largest difference between day and night time. There is a difference in the duration of a day (which is equal to 243 Earth days) and a year (which is equal to 225 Earth days)!"

Planets of Our Solar System

- **Mercury**
- **Venus**
- **Earth**
- **Mars**
- **Jupiter**
- **Saturn**
- **Uranus**
- **Neptune**

The Sun's gravitational pull keeps these planets in their orbits. Earth, being the third planet from the Sun, is considered the most suitable for life.

interesting fact: Jupiter's gravity is so powerful that it pulls in small asteroids and comets, protecting Earth from them.

Space

Space Travel Humans have already started traveling into space. The first human spaceflight was conducted by Yuri Gagarin in 1961. Nowadays, astronauts live in the ISS (International Space Station) and conduct various experiments there. Spacecrafts are used for space travel, which are capable of traveling beyond Earth.

Why is there no gravity in space, and why does it feel that way?

- Earth's Pull: We live on Earth. The Earth has a special force called gravity. This force pulls us towards the Earth, so we are able to stand on the ground.

- No Ground in Space: There is no ground in space. Therefore, the Earth's pull cannot be felt there. Spacecraft Also Revolves: The spacecraft revolves around the Earth. Just like a swing, the spacecraft also keeps revolving. That's why astronauts feel like they are floating in the air.

So does that mean there's no gravity in space? Not at all! There is gravity in space, but it's much weaker. The farther you go from Earth, the less the effect of gravity. But space is so vast that it seems to us that there is no gravity there. Let's understand this with an example: Suppose you throw a ball upwards. The ball comes back down after a while. This happens because the Earth's gravity pulls the ball towards it. But if you throw the ball very hard, it may escape the Earth's grip and go into space. Once in space, the effect of Earth's gravity on the ball will be very less and the ball will keep floating in space.

Interesting fact:

There is gravity in space, but it is very weak. Astronauts feel like they are floating in the air because the

Earth's pull is very weak there.

Black Hole

What is a black hole?

Imagine a super, super heavy star. When this star dies, it can collapse into a tiny, super dense point in space. This point is so heavy that its gravity pulls everything towards it, even light! That's why we call it a black hole. It's like a cosmic vacuum cleaner, sucking up everything around it!

Why can't we see black holes?

Since black holes suck in light, we can't actually see them. But we can see the effects they have on the stars and gas around them. Scientists use special telescopes to study this and learn more about black holes.

How big are black holes?

Black holes come in all sizes! Some are as small as a single atom, while others are millions of times bigger than our Sun.

Can a black hole swallow the Earth?

While it's true that black holes have a lot of gravity, the Earth is not in any danger of being swallowed up by one. The nearest black hole is very far away!

Introduction

Have you ever looked up at the night sky and wondered about the twinkling stars? Do you know what our Earth revolves around? Let's embark on an exciting journey through the solar system together. We will learn about the Sun, planets, moons, and much more. Do you know which is the biggest planet? Or which is the smallest? You will find answers to all these questions in this book. You will learn how important the Sun is to us. You will also learn about the appearance of other planets and what they are like. So let's start our journey!

Creative Section:

- Create your own planet and think about how it would look and what kind of creatures would live there!

- Imagine you are traveling to Mars. What things would you see there?

- If you were an astronaut, which planet would you visit and why?

Quiz

1.What is the name of our galaxy?
(a) Andromeda (b) Milky Way (c) Orion (d) Magellanic Cloud.

2.What type of star is the Sun?
(a) Red dwarf (b) Yellow dwarf (c) Blue supergiant (d) White dwarf.

3.Which is the largest planet in the solar system?
(a) Earth (b) Mars (c) Jupiter (d) Saturn.

4.Who was the first woman to go into space?
(a) Sally Ride (b) Kalpana Chawla (c) Valentina Tereshkova (d) Sunita Williams.

5.Who was the first person to walk on the Moon?

(a) Neil Armstrong (b) Buzz Aldrin (c) Michael Collins (d) Yuri Gagarin.

Quiz

6.What is a black hole? (a) A giant star (b) A place where gravity is so strong that even light cannot escape (c) A type of cloud (d) A spaceship.

7.What are comets made of? (a) Rock, dust, and ice (b) Rock only (c) Ice only (d) Dust only.

8.What are meteoroids? (a) Small pieces of rock that fall to Earth from space (b) Stars (c) Clouds (d) Mountains.

9.Which planet is called the Red Planet? (a) Mars (b) Jupiter (c) Saturn (d) Uranus.

10.How do astronauts breathe in space? (a) By drinking water (b) By wearing an oxygen mask (c) There is air in space (d) They don't breathe.

Answer:

- 1.(b) Milky Way
- 2.(b) Yellow dwarf
- 3.(c) Jupiter
- 4.(c) Valentina Tereshkova
- 5.(a) Neil Armstrong
- 6.(b) A place where gravity is so strong that even light cannot escape
- 7.(a) Rock, dust, and ice
- 8.(a) Small pieces of rock that fall to Earth from space
- 9.(a) Mars
- 10.(b) By wearing an oxygen mask

Puzzle

Unscramble the letters to find the name of a planet:

- **RAEMRCUY**
- **VENSU**
- **SRMA**
- **JUPITER**
- **SATURN**
- **URANUS**
- **NEPTUNE**

Answers:

- Mercury
- Venus
- Mars
- Jupiter
- Saturn
- Uranus
- Neptune

www.ingramcontent.com/pod-product-compliance
Lightning Source LLC
Chambersburg PA
CBHW061316170726
48282CB00020B/118